ALIENS –
THE NEVER ENDING STORY!
Stories of Close Encounters

Robyn P. Watts

KNOWLEDGE
BOOKS

Teacher Notes:

People have been fascinated by the idea of alien life for many years! You can find strange evidence of possible alien life from as far back as the Ancient Egyptian civilizations through to the present day. Join the author as she shares her own UFO encounter, shares other encounters from around the world, and talks about the science behind this amazing and never ending story.

Discussion Points for Consideration:

1. Why do you think the topic of alien life is so fascinating to people?

2. Why do you think there is so much confusion with UFO sightings?

3. How do you think the world would change if alien life existed?

Difficult words to be introduced and practiced before reading the book:

Ancient, encounters, unidentified, aerial, phenomenon, pyramids, impossible, understood, spacecraft, astronaut, horizon, hovered, disappeared, recorded, meteors, satellites, lightning, electricity, radar, operator, military, physical, hypnotized, proven, difficult, extra-terrestrial, aliens, universe, intelligent, technology, scientists, influencers, continue.

Contents

1. About UFOs and UAPs

Who has not read or heard a story about UFOs and UAPS? There are so many stories about aliens and space. What are UFOs and UAPs? A UFO means an Unidentified Flying Object. Scientists now call them UAPs. This means Unidentified Aerial Phenomenon.

People say they have seen flying objects, strange moving lights, and even strange beings. How many of these stories are true? We do not know the answer. If you see something strange, does that make it a UFO or UAP?

UAPs are not just seen in one area. Strange objects have been seen all over the world. There have been stories of strange objects and beings throughout history. Many people believe they have seen UAPs.

Not only are these UAPs seen across the world, but also back through history. There are stories of strange beings and objects in many stories. These UAPs were even seen in ancient times.

2. Ancient Encounters

Were UAPs present a long time ago? Did the Egyptians and ancient peoples see aliens? There are ancient paintings of figures with rays on their heads. Could these be aliens with shining lights? We can only guess!

In South America and Egypt, there are pyramids built with 100 ton stones. How did they move these stones using just people and animals? It seems impossible today that they were able to build these giant pyramids.

There are huge lines in the deserts of Peru in South America. These lines can only be understood from the sky. They are called the Nazca Lines and were made thousands of years ago.

The lines look like a long runway for aircraft. Aircraft did not exist back in those days. Were these runways for alien spacecraft? There are also lines showing animals and one that looks like an astronaut.

3. Types of Encounters

My story is one of many thousands of sightings. One day, just as the Sun had faded over the horizon, we saw strange lights. The lights moved slowly down amongst the trees in the forest. They were there for about five minutes.

A light suddenly moved into the valley and hovered. It glowed very bright, then moved so fast, and disappeared over the mountain.

That night we reported what we had seen to the local police. They said to check for aircraft in the area at the time of the sighting. The local airport said that no planes had been there.

People could not imagine seeing a bright light that changed and grew stronger. The light then moved away faster than any other object on Earth.

How are these sightings reported and recorded? A moving ball of light in the sky is a common sight and could be many things. It could be a jet plane moving across the sky.

When meteors crash to Earth, they give off light. Satellites are very common now and move across the sky. They can also fall back to Earth and give off a bright light.

A storm with lots of lightning can cause a fireball. This fireball is caused by electricity. The brightness can make it look like a single object.

Radar can show objects which are not really there. The radar operator can see balloons and planes on the screen and send a warning. People on the ground might see something strange and report it as a UFO. Other people then believe it to be a UFO.

Radar does make mistakes. It can show objects which appear and then disappear. This can be caused by storms and changes in weather.

A close encounter of the first kind is when you see a flying object. It must be less than 500 feet away. You must be able to see important things like lights and windows. You must be able to see more than just a ball of light.

The encounter is reported to the police and the military. It becomes a stronger story if other people also report it. Encounters of the first kind are very common.

Close encounters of the second kind are more serious. This involves more than just seeing an object. You must have some physical contact or signs, including:

- Your car may stop or start suddenly.

- A dog or cat may bark, look scared, or run away.

- A sudden change from cold to hot or hot to cold.

- A feeling of being frozen and not able to talk.

- Burnt ground near the object.

- Crushed grass or broken trees near the object.

- Chemicals on the ground.

All these signs have been talked about in different reports.

Close encounters of the third kind are very serious. This is a UFO encounter with another being. This being can be something like a human. It could be a robot or some other form of life. The being must come from the UFO.

This would be a very scary encounter. Imagine seeing an alien coming out of a spacecraft! There are people who have reported seeing this and told their story. These encounters have been seen by many people.

A close encounter of the fourth kind is when a human is taken by a UFO. The person might be taken by force or hypnotized. They may be reported missing before they are found again. The person may also report that they were taken by a UFO.

There are many cases of people being taken by UFOs. The problem is being able to prove it happened. There are no stories where many people have seen someone being taken. This makes it very hard to prove.

A close encounter of the fifth kind is contact with an extra-terrestrial, or ET. In this encounter, the person talks to an ET. This may be by speaking, phone messages, or by messages to your brain. The ET may give thoughts and ideas to the person.

How can this be proven? This is a very difficult problem as people can make up stories. Who will believe these stories? Without proof, the story is just a story. Some people may want to believe, but it is better to wait for proof.

4. The Westall Encounter

This encounter happened in 1966 at Westall High School in Melbourne, Australia. Some students were outside with their teacher when they saw some low flying metal disks. The children looked at the disks coming towards them, just above the trees.

One of the students panicked and ran back to class to tell the other students. There were many disks and they moved over the school. The children all said they had seen these strange metal disks.

What did the children see? Could it have been a weather balloon? The students had no idea what they had seen. The teachers were told not to talk about it. The army and police did not help to explain the sightings.

The principal told the students that they had seen nothing important. What do you think? Did the students make a mistake? It is a long time ago, but they still believe they saw UFOs.

5. Ariel School Encounter

Another encounter happened at a school in Ariel, near the city of Harare, Zimbabwe. There had been many reports of UFOs and the news was full of sightings.

This day, some teachers went outside after hearing loud noises from the playground. Some children had seen silver disks land in a field near the school. They saw beings near the spacecraft. Others said that their minds suddenly became full of thoughts.

What had the children seen? Many children had seen something in the field. Others who were outside and playing did not see anything. Why did some see the UFO while others did not?

The children were asked to draw what they had seen. Most of the drawings were the same. They had some form of encounter, but what was it? This is one of the strangest encounters on record and hard to explain.

6. Area 51

Area 51 is a military base in Nevada, in the USA. It is said to be where the US military keeps proof of a UFO crash. In 1951, it is believed that a UFO crashed in Roswell, New Mexico, and that aliens were found.

People have said that they saw parts of a UFO being removed. Others have claimed that they saw alien bodies. This story has been talked about for a very long time.

WARNING

U.S. Air Force Installation

It is unlawful to enter this area without permission of the Installation Commander.
Sec. 21, Internal Security Act of 1950; 50 U.S.C. 797

While on this Installation all personnel and the property under their control are subject to search.

WARNING!

NO TRESPASSING
AUTHORITY N.R.S. 207-200
MAXIMUM PUNISHMENT: $1000 FINE
SIX MONTHS IMPRISONMENT
OR BOTH
STRICTLY ENFORCED

PHOTOGRAPHY
OF THIS AREA
IS PROHIBITED

18 USC   795

The military claims it was not a UFO, but a weather balloon. They say that the parts being taken away were from this balloon. The military have always said that there was no wrecked spacecraft and no alien bodies.

What do you think happened at Area 51? There have been many movies and stories made about this mystery. Do some more reading and watch the video for more on Area 51.

6. The Silence

The Universe is so big, it is hard to think about. Our Sun and planets are in the Milky Way Galaxy. It's hard to believe that our galaxy has 100 billion Suns or stars. If we count the planets there may be 5 times this number – that's 500,000,000,000 planets!

How many galaxies are out there? There are 2 trillion galaxies out there – that's 2,000,000,000,000 galaxies. Some of these galaxies are 10 times the size of the Milky Way. Could any of these trillions of planets support life?

With so many planets and galaxies out there, why is there silence? If there is very smart life in the universe, why is there no contact? The intelligent life would have to travel for a long time, and faster than the speed of light.

Why would they want to be here? Are they hiding out on Earth? Would they come all the way from another star just to be a tourist? Are there aliens already here living among us?

SETI is the Search for Extraterrestrial Intelligence. We cannot visit other stars that are thousands of years away from Earth. We do not have the technology or the time. SETI searches by listening to the signals coming from outer space.

The SETI scientists listen and look for signals from other planets. Life on our Earth is very active. We give off signals called radio waves. Smart beings may be using radio waves to talk to each other. SETI listens and searches for these special radio waves. So far, they have not found signs of intelligent life.

Scientists don't usually become famous YouTubers or influencers. Why is this? Science is about the careful search for correct answers. Science doesn't guess – it looks at all the facts! The modern world is built on science, not on influencers.

A scientist works to find the correct answer. This may be right or wrong. Other scientists could come along and improve on the answer. We must measure the facts with UFO encounters. If we only have one person's story to go by, we need more facts. We do not say no, but we do not say yes either! We continue to collect data!

Word bank

Ancient

encounters

unidentified

aerial

phenomenon

pyramids

impossible

understood

spacecraft

astronaut

horizon

hovered

disappeared

recorded

meteors

satellites

lightning

electricity

radar

operator

military

physical

hypnotized

proven

difficult

extraterrestrial

aliens

universe

intelligent

technology

scientists

influencers

continue